797,885 Books

are available to read at

Forgotten Books

www.ForgottenBooks.com

Forgotten Books' App
Available for mobile, tablet & eReader

ISBN 978-1-333-64206-8
PIBN 10530007

This book is a reproduction of an important historical work. Forgotten Books uses state-of-the-art technology to digitally reconstruct the work, preserving the original format whilst repairing imperfections present in the aged copy. In rare cases, an imperfection in the original, such as a blemish or missing page, may be replicated in our edition. We do, however, repair the vast majority of imperfections successfully; any imperfections that remain are intentionally left to preserve the state of such historical works.

Forgotten Books is a registered trademark of FB &c Ltd.
Copyright © 2017 FB &c Ltd.
FB &c Ltd, Dalton House, 60 Windsor Avenue, London, SW19 2RR.
Company number 08720141. Registered in England and Wales.

For support please visit www.forgottenbooks.com

1 MONTH OF FREE READING

at

www.ForgottenBooks.com

By purchasing this book you are eligible for one month membership to ForgottenBooks.com, giving you unlimited access to our entire collection of over 700,000 titles via our web site and mobile apps.

To claim your free month visit:

www.forgottenbooks.com/free530007

* Offer is valid for 45 days from date of purchase. Terms and conditions apply.

English
Français
Deutsche
Italiano
Español
Português

www.forgottenbooks.com

Mythology Photography **Fiction** Fishing Christianity **Art** Cooking Essays Buddhism Freemasonry Medicine **Biology** Music **Ancient Egypt** Evolution Carpentry Physics Dance Geology **Mathematics** Fitness Shakespeare **Folklore** Yoga Marketing **Confidence** Immortality Biographies Poetry **Psychology** Witchcraft Electronics Chemistry History **Law** Accounting **Philosophy** Anthropology Alchemy Drama Quantum Mechanics Atheism Sexual Health **Ancient History Entrepreneurship** Languages Sport Paleontology Needlework Islam **Metaphysics** Investment Archaeology Parenting Statistics Criminology **Motivational**

AN ADDRESS

DELIVERED BEFORE

THE IRVING SOCIETY

OF

ST. JAMES COLLEGE,

FOUNTAIN ROCK, MARYLAND,

AT THE

PUBLIC CELEBRATION OF THE SOCIETY,

COMMENCEMENT WEEK, JULY 9, 1860.

---o---

BY REV. C. H. HALL, D. D.

---o---

PUBLISHED BY REQUEST.

WASHINGTON, D. C.
BUELL & BLANCHARD, PRINTERS.
1860.

AN ADDRESS

DELIVERED BEFORE

THE IRVING SOCIETY

OF

ST. JAMES COLLEGE,

FOUNTAIN ROCK, MARYLAND,

AT THE

PUBLIC CELEBRATION OF THE SOCIETY,

COMMENCEMENT WEEK, JULY 9, 1860.

———o———

BY REV. C. H. HALL, D. D.

———o———

PUBLISHED BY REQUEST.

WASHINGTON, D. C.
BUELL & BLANCHARD, PRINTERS.
1860.

IRVING HALL, *July* 11, 1860.

To Rev. Charles H. Hall:

DEAR SIR: In behalf of the Irving Society, we would respectfully request a copy of your Address, for publication.

We remain, with great respect,
GEORGE B. SHATTUCK,
GEORGE H. SHAFER,
W. G. HARRISON,
Committee.

To Messrs. George B. Shattuck, George H. Shafer, and W. G. Harrison:

GENTLEMEN: It gives me great pleasure to comply with your request; and wishing you success in your labors after eloquence and art, and commending you to God and the word of His grace,

I am yours, truly,
CHARLES H. HALL.

ST. JAMES COLLEGE, *July* 11, 1860.

Exchange
Peabody Inst., Balto.
Jan. -28

ADDRESS.

---o---

The ideas which we form of eloquence and of the orator, from fifteen to twenty-five years of age, are of no ordinary importance to us, for many long days after this interesting period of our life has passed away. Between the two dates of our common cycle of threescore and ten, which I have chosen, the profoundest wisdom has placed very much of the original of our after acts and principles. It is the seed-time of life. At fifteen we ordinarily begin to think and feel—feel possibly more than think—yet, after a sort, think, too. The sun of reason rises in fogs of sentiment, romance, and fancy. The individual *ego*, is rather surprised to find a new and strange light rising upon it. The boy discovers that there are other *egos*, other sentient circles of life, which will yet cross and contract his own. Hitherto he has lived as the butterflies, lighting by necessity on other supports at times, and with a shorter flight than his own imagination supposes, but with very little practical knowledge of the life around and before him. He can at any time fly away to the blue skies, and sail through the upper deeps on the floating clouds. And Hope has only half made up her mind to do so, when the time convenient for it comes, as come it must. He can be a poet if he will, and, for all he knows, he may yet choose to be. He can rise to the highest achievements of eloquence, and command the applause of listening senates; and he doubtless often ponders with himself the perplexing question, whether he will do so, or not; whether he will occupy the place of "His Majesty the President," as our Japan friends have lately styled him, or will sublimely yield the honor, only waiting for him to choose, and sail to other lands, to rival the fame of the few missionaries whose deeds are chronicled among men.

I frankly confess my admiration for all such boys. It is a glorious trick of fancy, that it thrills their young blood, and dignifies the nascent days of life with " a light and loveliness" that too soon pass away from earth. It is no shame that it is a delusion. Without such delusions, we are then only little animals. We grow, and may perhaps in time be very excellent citizens, but we shall walk a lower round of duty. The imagination is God's gift. It cheers the child; it gives a sacred repose to the old man. It fires us to exertion in our first efforts to put the carnal below the spiritual. It looks off the edge of time, when man has passed the dust and toil of his journey, and but for it would sink into listless indifference, and sees " a city without foundations," whose pearly gates are tinged by it with a splendor which warms the dull, chill blood of age, and lights him gently to his last sleep. If it deceives, it also reveals; if it tricks us, it is also inspired, and is the great dynamic force of all noble and glorious action. The child under the fir-tree, playing away his sunny hours, while the mystic chemistry of Nature is building up its secret wonders of bone and muscle in the growing form, thinks " their little tops are close against the sky." The man, indeed, learns better, but, as the poet says:

> " Finds it little joy
> To know he's farther off from heaven
> Than when he was a boy."

And the boy, till fifteen, loves romance, and dotes on sentiment; he loves Marmion, (terrible savage that he was,) or dreams with the Turk, in his guarded tent,

> " As wild of thought, and gay of wing,
> As Eden's garden bird."

Dream on! Let it not be my hand that wakes you, fair child! dream on! though the castle of thy hopes be as baseless as the fabric of a vision. Dream on! till some softer hand may stir the curls on thy brow, and possibly breathe to thee in the sweet music of love, with prattling voices in chorus, the knowledge that every man of us has something better to do in this world than dream.

After fifteen, a boy who has anything in him out of which to make a man, begins to awake to the necessities of his existence, both in his own soul and in the world outside of it, which he may wisely study. He may not be " President of these United States," though his nursery rhyme has taught him that its privileges would number among them an unbounded license over the residuum of the sugar cane, and an unusual vibration of the gates leading to the White House. He may not command listening senates without a vast amount of labor in advance, and not then by only a voice of thunder, impregnable logic, and rhetoric sweetly tuneful as the spheres. He may not even always trust to have the soft hand which now yields to his, or the undivided homage of the eyes which now speak very curious things to him. The stream of his life may ripple on banks of roses and nodding cowslips; but there is a swifter current becoming visible in it—a sound of far-off possibilities is mingling with its murmur, and the hot sun is up. He begins to see life as a problem for his solution. He wakes, to find in this land of ours some thirty millions of people, who have just his rights, just his modes of being, and just his hopes and fancies. Marmion, on his fiery war-horse, he begins to think, would do very ill in the streets of our cities. He would ride down our little ones, and run against—no knightly De Wilton with lance in rest, but only—the constable.*

He may rail at *the times*, in revenge, and sigh for " the good old days." Or he may jump the present, and sing of " a good time coming." But the very best time for us, the time that a Mind which rules this great world with infinite wisdom and love and beauty has fixed on as best for you and me, is just this blessed summer day, in the year of our Lord eighteen hundred and sixty. We cannot better it by sighs. We cannot go backward, nor can we hurry it. Let us to work, and use it.

" Trust no future, howe'er pleasant,
Let the dead past bury its dead;
Act, act in the living present,
Heart within, and God o'erhead."

How beautiful are these words of that quiet poet of Cambridge! How they have spoken out what is in ten myriad young souls! How reasonable, wise, and practical, they are! Let me, in the spirit of them, speak to you, young gentlemen, of the one theme for which I may rationally suppose that your debating society has been established, and of which you are wishing me now to say my say.

Your ideas of eloquence, from fifteen to twenty-five—pardon me if I venture to unveil the thoughts which are common to us all, yet which we do not quite choose to confess to each other. To do it, I must say, first of all, that I do it *reverently ;* that I go back on my own course, and, by a sleight of memory, join you in your seats, and listen while I speak.

What is Eloquence ? It is simply *out-speaking—e-loquor*, to speak out. It is human revelation; the bringing out the word which is a living reality in us; the living truth within, which men need, which they will receive, which they will reverence, which will win them, convince them, rule them; the word which will drive their bad passions scared into darkness; which will soothe their sorrows, check their anger, hush their riot, annul the icy touch of despair; the word which will

---

* Or an *omnibus*.—PRIN. DEV.

raise their courage, kindle afresh their energy, thrill their better soul, and give to all good and noble powers a new ascendency in the strife with the bad and base temptations around them. Eloquence is one single living word, spoken in season; vital in its birth, as it springs out of a soul in the act of labor; leaping out of a travailing brain, as Minerva from the head of Jove, in full armor, polished, glittering, terrible with spear and casque, able at once to do battle for right; a new creation in the fight of life; a living power, better and grander in its divine might and majesty than a regiment of men. Eloquence is the gift of God. It comes down from heaven, for it does not belong to the baser things of earth. It comes out of a soul, which, filled with holy thought, rises above us, and for the time utters *oracles* beyond gainsaying, and too glorious to be questioned.

Let me cite three instances in illustration of my faith, the better for my purpose that they are as commonly known among you as household words. Demosthenes, it it said, shook the throne of Philip, and held back for a time the destinies of Greece by his eloquence. He rose before his countrymen, and his mere words were supreme over them. The Macedonian terror for the time was forgotten.

Now, what may your fancies of him be? Shall I tell my own? They were possibly; why not do likewise now? If it has been done, it may be done again. If man has thus risen to a great, majestic victory, by the mere force of his single will, he may do it again. Let us shake the power of tyrants. Let us prepare, in dark cellars, and with mouths pebble-filled, for the day when the star-spangled banner shall be in danger; when we can rise before our trembling fellow-citizens, and with voice of semi-inspiration drive off the invading foe from our shores, and come back, in triumphal fashion, to honors and admiring myriads. The maidens and others shall raise their pæans, and shout, "Saul hath slain his thousands, but this fair and ruddy shepherd-boy his ten thousands."

Is there nothing of this delusive trickery in fancy? Eloquence is all that I have said; who, then, may not speak out? We will be eloquent! ah, wait a while; we have forgotten some things. This fancy is at the bottom of a ceaseless stream of what is called *spread-eagle* eloquence in this land of ours. It rings out abundantly, on the Fourth of July, from Maine to Georgia, as the drum-beat of parading soldiery; and, like theirs, the sound is very much produced by inflated skins of innocent sheep. Sundry things are beyond us. Thank God that they are beyond us. Thank God that before you can thus rise up to receive the meed of rescuing a nation, the nation must be in danger; men must be in grief, and you must grieve with the saddest of them; and our nation is not in grief.

There are demagogues, I know, who would see the fair fields of our land in peril, if it would give *them* the notoriety which would inevitably disgrace them. There are fancies working in the hot blood of many men, which, if indulged, would clothe the land in mourning. They would fain be even as Attila, "the scourge of God," and have the spot where their horse's hoof fell without vegetation forever, that they might march before the crowd, like the procession of a theatre, the observed of all observers.

But we leave Attila to our friend Carusi and his painted canvas, or if he should get out into the streets and begin a row, we hand him over to the police. Imagination needs the stimulus of ancient examples; and the young man without imagination can never be eloquent, for he can never *imagine* the wants of other men, nor feel in himself their griefs, and speak out the remedy for them. But we need something more. Philip of Macedon cannot now call forth his one Demosthenes. Philip can be better managed by Dahlgren guns and Minie balls. The age when one man could accomplish this potent fame was an age which we can no more reproduce now, than we can bring back the epoch of the Crusaders. The *one man day* is passed. It is drowned in printer's ink, and fettered with red tape. We must take our comfort for the change as we may, but for you and me, depend upon it, no Demosthenic era will ever dawn; or if it does, we shall mourn the triumph in profoundest sadness. I doubt not that he was the saddest man of all Greece. The words he uttered came from a man who had wept in a cellar, as well as studied periods there; had quailed before the ocean's roar before he compelled the wilder waves of human passion into silence. Eloquence—remember it well—is a stern, sober gift, as all spiritual things are. You must first learn in anguish to control your own heart, and its passions, before you can be worthy to control the souls of other men.

Another orator, whose facile-pen and Augustan age gave him the opportunity of directing the fancies and principles of men, in regard to his art, more than any single man, was Cicero. And though Cicero has left orations far superior in grace and finish to the four against Catiline; in my opinion, he culminated as an orator in the first of these four. The defence of Milo reads better; but in the one he was an orator, in the other he was a graceful coward. In the one case he spake as a hero; in the other, he trembled before the base minions of Clodius. In the one, he deserved a place among the gods of his country's Pantheon; in the other, he almost merited a cell in the Mammertine prison. Let us recall the vision of his glory.

It was a fair Italian day without; but Rome was a moral

earthquake, just ready to burst out. Terrible thoughts scared men; women and children were palsied with fear. The most awful hour of a country's history was upon them, and at any moment the cry of horror might arise, to tell that the curse had fallen. The Senate assembled; and Catiline, wily, skilful, cautious, civil, sedate, honorable, and scrupulous Catiline, whose hellish wisdom had warily worn the garb of legal blamelessness, came into the Senate-house to take his honorable seat with the rest. Why not? Who of all the Senators there could unravel the meshes of his plot? Who of them could dive into the pestilential vaults of his dark soul, and unearth the Guy Fawkes, and betray the secret train which was to blow that Senate to the winds. He had done no single thing which a common mind could seize upon, and charge upon him as a certain evidence of guilt. He is smiling as he walks. He will take his seat and join in the debate, and by the sunset he will raise his standard, and bring the head of accursed, prattling Cicero, to the earth in death. Go, and read again the debate in Sallust, and see the difficulty of the position on that memorable day.

Cicero dashed upon him with a divine impulse. He seems, for once, to have forgotten himself. He tracks the plot step by step, he rouses the fears, the patriotism, the indignation, of his auditors. The marble statues seem to nod to his eye. He almost raves with inspiration, as if the immortal gods of Rome had taken possession of him for the time, and hid the orator in the patriot. He scorches the traitor by his vehement, resistless zeal, and drives him from the city, howling curses as he flies. He had conquered him, and dispersed the cloud by that one oration, and saved his country.

It was a glorious achievement of manliness, state-craft, art, and eloquence. I pardon him, that he could never all forget it. A man who has once been filled with so divine an impulse might well believe that it was something more than an individual triumph.

And may not boys be pardoned too, if, as they spell out "Quousque tandem, O Catilina," they catch the fiery impulse, and long to do and dare as he did; if they suffer tricksy fancy to build a senate chamber, and people it with citizens of honor, (not forgetting the smiling galleries,) and long for the day when they shall rise in their seats, and stop some giant evil in its hour of success, roll back the tide of ruin from the land, unearth the secret villainy, and drive away from the sacred deposit of our Constitution the wicked hands which are about to destroy it?

Allow me to hope that in our time no one of you may have this distinguished privilege—to suggest, that exciting as the triumph of another such orator as Cicero might be, the presence of his Catiline had better be spared. For, though Cicero was the honored saviour of his country, he saved it but for a short time. The fire of his eloquence was soon to expire. It graced a crumbling government. It is far better to read of him, and his friend Cato, and his rival Julius Cæsar, than to have them here among us. Put them in our Senate Chamber, and they would be at bowie knives or pistols, by way of persuasive arguments. And possibly the boys who do resort to those rhetorical arts in that building, have once, in bygone days, fancied in their turn that they would be as patriotic as he was, and have found out their mistake before this. They rise in their seats to scorch each other, and promise to reveal depths of corruption, at which Catiline would wonder as an innocent babe; but somehow our Catilines do not run from the revelation, and our Ciceros sound very tame, as we read their philippics in the *Daily Globe*.

But in all earnestness let me say to you, that it is a vain fancy to read history, as if such scenes as it offers could be again enacted. Our *bema* is no more that of a Cicero, than our country is a Rome. If eloquence is *out-speaking*, it is what *we* have to say, what belongs to our nineteenth century; and we must say that which is within *us*, not what was in the old Romans.

Again let me bid you note, that eloquence is no holiday thing. Pleasant as it is for me to stand here, and look over your young faces, and join you for the time in your festive hours, it will be fruitless, if I cannot impress upon you that eloquence is your whole self speaking, your whole self so engaged that for the time you forget yourself, and the whole soul burns before your hearers. And *burning* is not pleasant.

This reminds me of an anecdote, which may not be dignified, but will certainly be illustrative. There was in one of our cities a "sensation preacher." This class of people are the most luckless of our citizens. Avoid them as you would the plague. He was brilliant, dazzling, noisy, and crowds flocked to hear him.

Now, as I read the New Testament, and human life, the preacher's eloquence is honest out-speaking of the Gospel, as he knows it. A great light shines in his own soul, and he cannot keep it in—and so out it comes; it comes out as semi-inspired teaching. It is an earnest, simple, straight-forward work, to say to men what men ought to hear, and mostly say it in plain American. But a sensation preacher is a mingling of the Ciceronian with Massillon, Whitefield, and honest old Peter Cartwright, who himself is not one of this race. He aims at a scene, and even the most abstract dogma of his sect becomes suddenly dramatic, and struts or dances with galvanic life before us, as he beats the Bible, and " tears a passion to tatters."

The individual of whom I speak was a thief—not as bad as Judas, but an eclectic thief, and not one of whom the police could take notice; he simply dressed himself in other men's thoughts. An old man came with the crowd to hear him, and sat beneath the pulpit. As an orotund passage rolled over his head, he muttered, half audibly, " That's Doddridge!" another came—" That's South!" another—" That's Chalmers." The preacher heard and felt the blows; and, leaning over the pulpit in a rage, burst out upon him in a violent and vulgar invective. The old man, without moving a limb, simply responded as before, " That's *his own !*" And that which is *our own* is our eloquence. It is the man who speaks out, and the man is not the tongue, nor the thought only, not often the man we pretend, but the real man, the heart, the life, the courage, the honest, genuine, outspoken man himself. When Cicero withered Catiline, the whole man shone in light. When he trembled before the faction of Clodius, the sweetly modulated logic and polished rhetoric of the oration " *Pro Milone,*" do not save us from a feeling of contempt. Let us not forget, in justice to him, that he was not always so—that he also wrote, like the bayings of a wounded lion, the philippics against Anthony— which cost him, and he knew the price as he wrote them—his head.

What you have to learn is, that in this American life of ours, we want to hear *the man*. We will not put up with shams, except in pulpits. We want men to speak out. If the voice is sweet as a summer wind, or rolling as muttering thunders, in great diapason tones of harmony, well. If the logic is the result of long and arduous training, until it plants its blows between the very eyes of a subject, terse, rapid, Heenan-like, better; if the rhetoric be, as among us, only an Everett can effect, better still; if the fancy flit along the line of discourse, revealing whole avenues of co-ordinate thought, and suggesting more than it speaks, better yet. But behind all, above and through all this, the orator of this land must speak out what is in him. The power to do this is the power divine.

I find one man who has been able to do this in our country. Others did it, and do it, for I am no skeptic of my country's glory. She produces, at the right moment, just the man, or men, which are wanted, whether to scale the walls of Monterey, fight the icebergs of the Pole, or unlock the gates of Japan. And they know well how to speak the word they want, whether it be to say, "We have met the enemy, and they are ours!" or to sow "a little more grape" on the plains of Buena Vista. But we have had, as Greece and Rome had, in the times of the two men I have mentioned, our crisis, and our Heaven-sent man to meet it; a man of whom Thomas Jefferson has said, "that he was the greatest orator that ever lived:" to whom he has awarded a praise even higher, in his estimation, that "he certainly gave the first impulse to the ball of the Revolution."* He took a part of his education with a fishing-rod in his hand, and studied his eloquence very much from the running brooks. A difficult and dangerous school is this, young gentlemen. You need not pay tuition at it, or it will be paid you again in tears and vain regrets. You will be as foolish to do so, as one would be to ride out on the country roads to-night, and practice the part of Rob Roy McGregor, which Wordsworth says was

"The good old rule—the simple plan,
That they should get who have the power,
And they should keep who can."

The youth who rises upward, breaks through necessity, conquers disadvantages, and meets a great occasion with the eloquent power of majestic self-possession, is of another stuff from the sentimentalist, who is recreant to his duties, neglects his privileges, and comes back from his profound studies in the woods and by the brooks, a trifling, sickly, and rheumatic sciolist. The training which a man may have at a plough-handle or a blacksmith's anvil may fit him for honored deeds, because of the mental energy and the moral habits really so trained; but the energy and the training are not magic gifts of ploughs or anvils.

But be this as it may. One hundred years ago, England and America were beginning to feel the throes of a coming revolution. Great wildernesses and Indian fights had cut in upon the European ideas of our ancestors. Loyalty grew sick and pined, three thousand miles from home, and neglected at that. The King had sold the country, and forgotten it. His statesmen were quite too busy with other things, to cast a care across the broad Atlantic. Men had cut down forests and cleared lands, and planted corn and tobacco, and fought "red devils," the best they could. In doing so, without any assistance from home, they somehow discovered that they could do it and dispense with help. They had occasional aid, and Braddock came over to deploy splendidly in swamps, where he made very sad work of it. Marmion might as well have arrayed his band in steel harness, and charged on their red foes. Men thenceforward distrusted the old feudalism the more. They had some things

---

* Wirt's Life of Patrick Henry, pp. 54, 59.

to do in Massachusetts and Virginia, which could not be learned in Oxford, or at the Court of St. James. And they were men grown, self-reliant and independent, before they dreamed that any sinner could ever think of defying the authority over them of his Majesty by the grace of God, King George the Third. Following the plough and wielding the axe, they had strong muscles; trailing the war-path and swimming rivers, they had good wind; "sighting" Indians and other "varmint" around forest trees and through jackvines, they had an unpleasant knack of the rifle and tomahawk. And thus Nature had put them all to school; and they were big boys, and only did not know that feudalism, like the malaria, could not cross salt water, and that they were men, with certain inalienable rights, which no power on earth could ever take from them.

But they began to produce wealth in the Colonies, and the mother country at once became anxious for their moral regimen. She proposed to send over her kindly lessons of wisdom, and train her forest children in the way they should go, by taxes and other testimonies of her interest; but she was an age too late.

Yet, in Virginia especially, the altered condition of the two people was singularly hindered by many circumstances from being declared openly. Little lords here still aped the manners of lords at home, and pride and aristocracy flourished on the plantations and in the towns of James river and the Rappahannock. The New England Puritans could speak out their complaints, and no thanks to them. They had learned to do so in nasal tones before they left Delft Haven. But the "Old Dominion" was loyal; good or bad, she could not quite forget the time when, despite the successes of Cromwell's Roundheads, she had remained bravely loyal to Church and King.

You may imagine the crisis without my description. It was at its climax, when there walked into the old Raleigh Tavern, at Williamsburgh, a tall, thin man, "dressed in very coarse apparel," with a series of resolutions in view before him, (though written by himself, to be presented by an aristocratic neighbor,) to say the word which then seethed in all men's minds, and yet none dared utter it. The aristocrats were perplexed; they felt it coming, but they dared not yet, without a farther provocation, break away from the sacred ties of home, and peril all. No; it wanted a man of Nature—a man of the *tiers etat*—a plebeian—who had not so much to lose as to give him a moment's pause, whose whole soul could kindle with the tremendous word then in the hearts of all, and though its utterance would cost him not only the countenance of his friends and acquaintances, but possibly his head too, would not fear or falter, as he set the ball in motion, and sent over the earth the one great, imperishable American word, which shall live forever, in all human hearts—the word *Independence*.

I confess to a child's admiration for the scenic effect of that birth-hour of liberty, as described in the history of his life. Says Wirt: " The cords of argument, with which his adversaries frequently flattered themselves that they had bound him fast, became packthreads in his hands. He burst them with as much ease as Samson did the bands of the Philistines. He seized the pillars of the temple, shook them terribly, and seemed to threaten his opponents with ruin. It was an incessant storm of lightning and thunder, which struck them aghast. The faint-hearted gathered courage from his countenance, and cowards became heroes, while they gazed upon his exploits." *

The excitement was at its height in 1765, when Patrick Henry uttered the famous words—" Cæsar had his Brutus, Charles the First his Cromwell, and George the Third "—what! Shall he dare to finish the sentence? Shall he pollute our aristocratic and loyal ears by it? No. " Treason ! " cried the Speaker. " Treason " came from every side of the House. Henry, rising to his full height, *did not say it ;* but the very *not saying* was the most tremendous utterance possible of what all then felt. He added, with firmest emphasis—" may profit by their example. If that be treason, make the most of it." He led all men by this siopesis just to the edge of a precipice, and showed them what was yawning beneath them. It was one flash of lightning, striking nowhere, killing no one, crossing no law, nothing treasonable spoken, but flashing off into the depths below, and revealing them. Every man in Williamsburgh that night pictured to himself how that sentence was destined to be finished. It was a glorious scene, a purely American scene, the first ellipsis between the two points of which was cradled *the Revolution.*

Would you have done it? Fancy may say to you what she will, but I will conclude with a few kindly words of advice, and thank you for your attention. I have spoken to you of the dreams of the unchastened imagination, in the years when fancy stands sidewise, and " conceals every thorn, but reveals every flower." Let me not be supposed to intend simply discouragement of such dreams. Much that is in them will perish ; but they indicate great truths. The simple problem—and how important—is to see these dreams change happily into solid, useful, practical life; to find, as the unreal light has passed away, it has given place to a sounder, grander, holier light, in all our consciousness.

---

* Wirt's Life of Patrick Henry, page 83.

If I have defined eloquence aright, the first corollary from my argument is plain—be all that you mean to speak out. There will, I trust, and you should not doubt, be noble hours in the future for you all—hours when the words which you may be called to utter, from an honest heart and well-trained mind, moved upon by powers almost consciously above your own control, may be winged with wonderful might and majesty to others. To be ready for such hours, is your work—is God's gift. To say those words, you have two lines of duty and work—one to cultivate assiduously all the arts of graceful, correct, and musical utterance; the other to cultivate, in the fear of God, in reverence for your work, and in patient endurance, that inner man, which is, at such moments, *to speak out*.

Eloquence is serious work. It is the sum, the issue, the aroma of life, the sweet fragrance of the healthy, living, patriotic and virtuous soul. Bushels of roses wither and die, to distil only a few drops of their precious attar, which enchants all. The rules of elocution are often confounded with it, or at least supposed to be the sufficient preparation for it. They bear about the same relation to it that the cradle does to the infant, or the schoolmaster's rod to the boy, it helps to discipline. They are necessary instruments, useful to an end, then very usefully forgotten. Demosthenes had to use pebbles, and depend upon it, you must work. You may as well undertake to sing the *Stabat Mater* or the *Miserere* without a maestro, as to gain command over the voice without mastery of elocution. The voice is the most delicate, arbitrary instrument in the world. You may carelessly abuse it, and damage all ears. You may choke it, stifle it; you may howl or shriek or mutter with it, and find enough to do it with you; but if you will speak out to any purpose, you must patiently learn to do it in clear, wholesome, easy, natural, orotund, resonant speaking. The power to do this is very rare among our people.

You must study language as the vehicle of your own thought—all the powers and possibilities of the words you are constantly using. You must purify your daily speech by the rules of good taste and courtesy. As a swearer lets slip an oath, so a vulgar mind shows its coarseness, insensibly. You must store the mind with all kinds of useful knowledge which it can healthily digest, nor be satisfied with any study until you begin to think upon it yourself—until it begins to be suggestive.

And then, beyond all else, you must cultivate the whole man. Be honest, be true to nature, to your country, and to God. Scorn mean and little and bad things. Rise to that position that you do nothing and think nothing that you are ashamed of. Be pure, that the Father of all may be pleased to touch your lips with fire. The palsying touch of unbelief in honor and nobility in man, is on our land. Rise above it, by having that in you which you would see or rouse in others. Then, even if you are not called to command Senates or to sway astonished multitudes, you may comfort yourself that you can speak out and compass all the legitimate objects of manly ambition. You may speak words to men as you find them, which shall be living principles. You may cultivate the eloquence which has fame and reward beyond the confines of time—the outspeaking of a soul trained, exalted, and purified, by its diviner powers and gifts.

I leave with you three maxims of eloquence—one from each of the orators of whom I have spoken. Ponder them. If rightly conceived, they contain whole essays of thought.

Demosthenes once being asked, wherein the secret of eloquence lay, replied, "*action*," or rather, in its best sense, "*acting, acting, acting;*" not the acting of the stage-player, nor the acting of the hypocrite, but the *being* for the time that which you represent.

Cicero has a famous contrast, only partly true, as violent contrasts always are, in the proverb, "*Poeta nascitur, orator fit*"—the orator *becomes*. He grows, by labor and the healthy growth of all his powers, up to his position of command.

And on the back of the original copy of those Virginia resolutions concerning the Stamp act, Patrick Henry wrote in later years, as the result of his own recollections of them, and his experience of men: * " Reader, whoever thou art, remember this, and in thy sphere, practice virtue thyself, and encourage it in others."

Wirt's Life of Patrick Henry, page 76.

CPSIA information can be obtained
at www.ICGtesting.com
Printed in the USA
LVHW041139121118
596800LV00004B/860

9 781333 642068